初級日本語
［げんき］

AN INTEGRATED COURSE IN
ELEMENTARY JAPANESE

げんき

GENKI

I

ワークブック
WORKBOOK

Eri Banno 坂野永理
Yutaka Ohno 大野裕
Yoko Sakane 坂根庸子
Chikako Shinagawa 品川恭子

The Japan Times

First edition: February 2000
34th printing: May 2006

Editorial assistance: guild
Illustrations: Noriko Udagawa
Cover art and Editorial design: Nakayama Design Office
Gin-o Nakayama, Mutsumi Satoh, and Masataka Muramatsu
Published by The Japan Times, Ltd.
5-4, Shibaura 4-chome, Minato-ku, Tokyo 108-0023, Japan
Phone: 03-3453-2013
http://bookclub.japantimes.co.jp/
http://genki.japantimes.co.jp/

ISBN4-7890-1001-5

Printed in Japan

はじめに

　このワークブックはテキスト『初級日本語　げんき』の補助教材として使われることを目的として作られました。文法の練習をはじめ、聞く練習、漢字の練習などがあり、テキストで勉強した後、このワークブックを使い、学習項目の定着をはかることができます。

　本書の「会話・文法編」には、テキストで導入された各文法項目につき1ページのワークシートがあります。英語から日本語に翻訳する練習、絵を見て文を作る練習、穴埋め練習、質問に自由に答える練習などがありますが、既習の文法項目や単語も復習できるように出題されています。

　さらに、総合的な練習として、各課の最後に「聞く練習」のワークシートがあります。1つの課につき、会話文を中心として3つまたは4つの問題がCDに収録されていますので、それを聞いてワークシートの質問に答えてください。問題にはその課で導入された文法項目や単語が含まれていますので、課の学習項目をすべて修了した後に行ったほうがいいでしょう。

　「読み書き編」は、漢字の練習シートと漢字の穴埋め問題で構成されています（『げんきⅠ』のワークブックには英文和訳もあります）。漢字の導入後、書き方を覚えるまで、この漢字練習シートを使って何度も書いてみましょう。まず、その漢字のバランスを意識して、薄く書かれている漢字をなぞってみます。筆順はテキストの漢字表を参考にしてください。それから、そのモデルになるべく似せて書く練習をしましょう。

　漢字の穴埋め問題は、文章の中に漢字や熟語が意味のあるものとして組み込まれていますから、穴埋めをする前に必ず文章全体を読んでください。

　『げんきⅠ』の英文和訳の練習では、習った漢字をできるだけ使って文を書いてみましょう。

Preface

This workbook is designed as supplementary material for the textbook *Genki: An Integrated Course in Elementary Japanese.* It contains grammar exercises as well as listening practice and practice for kanji, and reinforces what was taught in each lesson of the textbook.

The Dialogue and Grammar section in this book contains a worksheet for each grammar point introduced in the textbook. The sheets include such exercises as translating English into Japanese, expressing the given pictures in Japanese, filling in the blanks, and answering open-end questions. Exercises are provided in such a way that students can also review the previously taught grammar items and vocabulary.

A worksheet for comprehensive listening practice is provided at the end of each lesson. It requires students to listen to three or four dialogues on the CD, and to answer questions on the sheet. These exercises should be carried out at the end of each lesson because the dialogues include a number of the study points from the lesson.

The Reading and Writing section consists of kanji worksheets and fill-in-the-blank type questions about the kanji. (Vol. 1 also includes English-Japanese translations.) Newly introduced kanji should be written over and over on the sheet until memorized. First, trace the lightly printed kanji samples, paying attention to the balance of the characters. For stroke order, refer to the kanji chart in the textbook. Continue by copying kanji into the blank boxes.

For the fill-in-the-blank questions about kanji, students should read through the whole sentences before filling in the blanks in order to learn kanji in context. For the English-Japanese translations in Vol. 1, students are encouraged to use previously taught kanji as much as possible.

げんき①ワークブック●もくじ

会話・文法編
かいわ　ぶんぽう　へん

あいさつ ■ Greetings

▶ What are these people saying? Write in Japanese the appropriate expression for each situation.

1. _____　　2. _____

3. _____　　4. _____

5. _____　　6. _____

7. _____

8. _____

9. _____

10. _____

11. _____

12. _____

13. _____

14. _____

第1課 1 Numbers
だい いっ か

▶ Write the following numbers in Arabic numerals.

(1) ご   五

(2) ぜろ   _____

(3) きゅう   _____

(4) さん   _____

(5) なな   七

(6) に   三

(7) ろく   九

(8) いち   ＼

(9) はち   _____

(10) よん   四

(11) じゅうろく   _____

(12) よんじゅう   _____

(13) にじゅういち   _____

(14) ひゃくろくじゅうよん   _____

(15) きゅうじゅうに   _____

(16) さんじゅうご   _____

(17) ななじゅうろく   _____

(18) じゅうはち   _____

(19) ひゃくごじゅうなな   _____

(20) ひゃくいち   _____

クラス ＿＿＿＿＿＿＿＿＿＿＿
(Class)

なまえ ＿＿＿＿＿＿＿＿＿＿＿＿＿＿＿＿＿＿＿＿＿
(Name)

第1課 2 Time and Telephone Numbers
だい いっ か

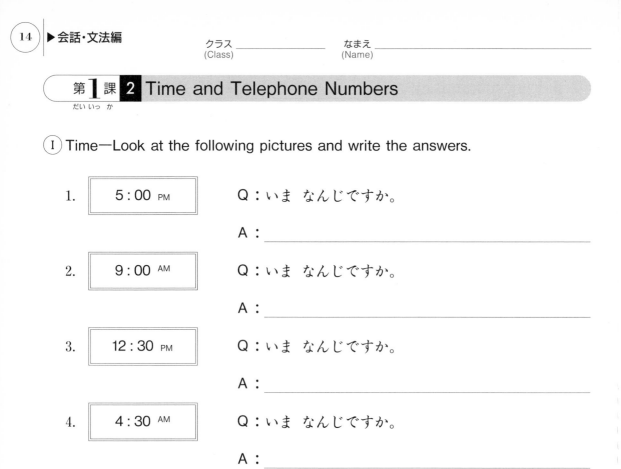

Ⅰ Time—Look at the following pictures and write the answers.

1. | 5 : 00 PM |

    Q：いま なんじですか。

    A：＿＿＿＿＿＿＿＿＿＿＿＿＿＿＿＿＿＿＿＿＿＿

2. | 9 : 00 AM |

    Q：いま なんじですか。

    A：＿＿＿＿＿＿＿＿＿＿＿＿＿＿＿＿＿＿＿＿＿＿

3. | 12 : 30 PM |

    Q：いま なんじですか。

    A：＿＿＿＿＿＿＿＿＿＿＿＿＿＿＿＿＿＿＿＿＿＿

4. | 4 : 30 AM |

    Q：いま なんじですか。

    A：＿＿＿＿＿＿＿＿＿＿＿＿＿＿＿＿＿＿＿＿＿＿

Ⅱ Telephone Numbers—Ask three people what their phone numbers are and write down the numbers in both Japanese and Arabic numerals.

1. ＿＿＿＿＿＿＿＿＿＿＿＿＿＿＿＿＿＿＿＿＿＿＿＿＿＿
(Arabic numerals:)

2. ＿＿＿＿＿＿＿＿＿＿＿＿＿＿＿＿＿＿＿＿＿＿＿＿＿＿
(Arabic numerals:)

3. ＿＿＿＿＿＿＿＿＿＿＿＿＿＿＿＿＿＿＿＿＿＿＿＿＿＿
(Arabic numerals:)

第1課 3 Noun₁の noun₂・X は Y です
だい いっ か

Ⓘ Translate the following phrases into Japanese using the framework "A の B." Note carefully that the order in which the two nouns appear may be different in English and in Japanese. Read Grammar 3 (pp. 16-17).

1. Japanese student　　　　　＿＿＿＿＿＿＿＿＿＿＿＿＿＿＿＿＿＿＿＿

2. Takeshi's telephone number　＿＿＿＿＿＿＿＿＿＿＿＿＿＿＿＿＿＿＿

3. My friend　　　　　　　　＿＿＿＿＿＿＿＿＿＿＿＿＿＿＿＿＿＿＿＿

4. English-language teacher　　＿＿＿＿＿＿＿＿＿＿＿＿＿＿＿＿＿＿＿

5. Michiko's major　　　　　　＿＿＿＿＿＿＿＿＿＿＿＿＿＿＿＿＿＿＿

Ⓘ Using the framework "X は Y です," translate the following sentences into Japanese.

1. Ms. Ogawa is Japanese.

＿＿＿＿＿＿＿＿＿＿＿ は ＿＿＿＿＿＿＿＿＿＿＿＿＿＿＿＿ です。

2. Mr. Takeda is a teacher.

3. I am an international student.

4. Michiko is a first-year student.

5. Ms. Yamamoto is 25 years old.

6. My major is Japanese.

第1課 4 Question Sentences
だい いっ か

Ⓘ Ask the right questions in each of the following exchanges.

1. You：　_____

　　Kimura：よねんせいです。

2. You：　_____

　　Kimura：れきしです。

3. You：　_____

　　Kimura：じゅうきゅうさいです。

4. You：　_____

　　Kimura：よんさんの ろくきゅういちななです。

5. You：　　すみません、いま _____

　　Kimura：いま くじはんです。

Ⅱ Translate the following sentences into Japanese.

1. Are you a student?

　　Yes, I am a student at Nihon University.

2. Is Michiko a fourth-year student?

　　No, Michiko is a third-year student.

クラス _____ (Class)
なまえ _____ (Name)

第1課 5 きくれんしゅう (Listening Comprehension)
だい いっ か

Ⓐ Listen to the CD and choose the correct picture below. 🔊 Disk1-17

1. (   ) 2. (   ) 3. (   ) 4. (   ) 5. (   ) 6. (   )

7. (   ) 8. (   ) 9. (   ) 10. (   ) 11. (   )

(a)

(b)

(c)

(d)

(e)

(f)

(g)

(h)

(i)

(j)

(k)

Ⓑ Listen to the dialogues between a passenger and a flight attendant in an airplane. Find out the times of the following cities. 🔊 Disk1-18

Word you may not know: どういたしまして。(You are welcome.)

Example: とうきょう   8:00 A.M.

1. パリ (Paris)
   ぱ り   _____

2. ソウル (Seoul)
   そ う る   _____

3. ニューヨーク (New York)
   に ゅ う よ お く   _____

4. ロンドン (London)
   ろ ん ど ん   _____

5. タイペイ (Taipei)
   た い ぺ い   _____

6. シドニー (Sydney)
   し ど に い   _____

Ⓒ Listen to the dialogues between Mr. Tanaka and a telephone operator. Find out the telephone numbers of the following people. 🔊 Disk1-19

Example: すずき   51-6751

1. かわさき   _____

2. リー (Lee)
   り い   _____

3. ウッズ (Woods)
   う っ ず   _____

4. トンプソン (Thompson)
   と ん ぷ そ ん   _____

Ⓓ Two international students, Lee and Taylor, are talking with a Japanese person. Listen to the dialogues and fill in the chart below. 🔊 Disk1-20

	1. Nationality	2. University	3. School Year	4. Major
Lee				
Taylor				

第2課 1 Numbers
だい に か

Ⅰ) Write the following numbers in Arabic numerals.

(1) よんひゃくななじゅう　_____

(2) はっぴゃくごじゅうさん　_____

(3) せんさんびゃく　_____

(4) いちまんななせん　_____

(5) さんぜんろっぴゃくじゅうに　_____

(6) ごせんひゃくきゅうじゅうはち　_____

(7) よんまんろくせんきゅうひゃく　_____

(8) きゅうまんにひゃくじゅう　_____

Ⅱ) Write the following numbers in *hiragana*.

1. 541　_____

2. 2,736　_____

3. 8,900　_____

4. 12,345　_____

Ⅲ) Look at the pictures and complete the dialogues.

¥160　　　¥24,000　　　¥3,600

1. Q : _____

   A : にまんよんせんえんです。

2. Q : かばんは いくらですか。

   A : _____

3. Q : しんぶんは いくらですか。

   A : _____

第2課 ② これ, それ, and あれ
だいにか

Ⅰ Mary and Takeshi are talking. Look at the picture and fill in これ, それ, or あれ.

メアリー：1.＿＿＿＿＿＿＿＿ は たけしさんの かさですか。

たけし：　いいえ、2.＿＿＿＿＿＿＿＿ は みちこさんの かさです。3.＿＿＿＿＿＿＿＿

　　　　　は メアリーさんの さいふですか。

メアリー：ええ、わたしの さいふです。たけしさん、4.＿＿＿＿＿＿＿＿ は たけし

　　　　　さんの じてんしゃですか。

たけし：　ええ、そうです。

メアリー：5.＿＿＿＿＿＿＿＿ は なんですか。

たけし：　ゆうびんきょくです。

Ⅱ Translate the following sentences into Japanese.

1. This is my bag.

2. (*Pointing at a thing near the listener*) That is Takeshi's book.

3. (*Pointing at a building 50 meters away*) That is a library.

4. (*Pointing at the dish in front of you*) Is this meat?

5. (*Pointing at a building 50 meters away*) What is that?

第2課 3 この, その, and あの・だれの
だいにか

Ⅰ Complete the following conversation between the attendant and the customer at a watch shop.

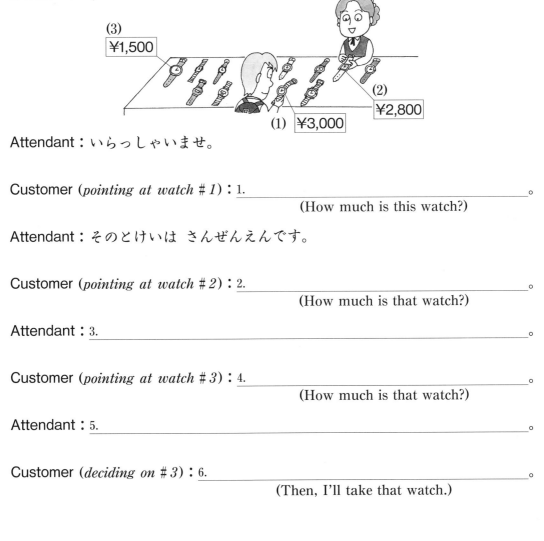

(3) ¥1,500
(2) ¥2,800
(1) ¥3,000

Attendant：いらっしゃいませ。

Customer (*pointing at watch #1*)：1. _____ 。
(How much is this watch?)

Attendant：そのとけいは さんぜんえんです。

Customer (*pointing at watch #2*)：2. _____ 。
(How much is that watch?)

Attendant：3. _____ 。

Customer (*pointing at watch #3*)：4. _____ 。
(How much is that watch?)

Attendant：5. _____ 。

Customer (*deciding on #3*)：6. _____ 。
(Then, I'll take that watch.)

Ⅱ Ask the right questions based on the underlined parts.

1. Q：_____ 。

A：それは たけしさんの じてんしゃです。

2. Q：_____ 。

A：(このくつは) きょうこさんの くつです。

クラス _____ なまえ _____

第2課 4 Noun も
だいにか

▶ Translate the following sentences into Japanese. Use も after the underscored phrases.

1. Ms. Tanaka is Japanese. <u>Mr. Yoshida</u> is Japanese, too.

2. Ms. Tanaka is twenty years old. <u>Mr. Yoshida</u> is twenty years old, too.

3. This dictionary is 2,000 yen. <u>That dictionary</u> is 2,000 yen, too.

4. This is my bicycle. <u>That</u> is my bicycle, too.

5. This is a Japanese book. <u>This</u> is a Japanese book, too.

6. Takeshi's major is history. <u>My major</u> is history, too.

7. Ms. Tanaka is a student at Nihon University. <u>Mr. Yoshida</u> is a student at Nihon University, too.

8. (A sentence of your own, describing two similar things/people.)

第2課 5 Noun じゃありません
だいにか

▶ Answer the following questions in the negative. These are all personal questions. "○○" (read まるまる) stands for your name. You will want to replace it with わたし in your answers.

1. すみません。たけしさんですか。

2. ○○さんは かいしゃいん (office worker) ですか。

3. ○○さんは にほんじんですか。

4. ○○さんの せんもんは れきしですか。

5. ○○さんは じゅうななさいですか。

6. これは ○○さんの じてんしゃですか。

7. それは ○○さんの かさですか。

8. すみません。あれは きっさてんですか。

第**2**課 **6** きくれんしゅう (Listening Comprehension)
だい に か

Ⓐ Listen to the dialogue at a kiosk and find out the prices of the following items. If you can't find out the price, indicate such with a question mark (?). 🔊 Disk1-30

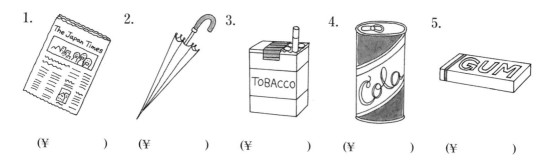

1.   2.   3.   4.   5.

(¥   )   (¥   )   (¥   )   (¥   )   (¥   )

Ⓑ Mary introduces her friend to Takeshi. Listen to the dialogue and fill in the blanks. 🔊 Disk1-31

Mary's friend's name is 1. _____. She comes from 2. _____.

She studies 3. _____ at the University of Paris.

Her mother is 4. _____. Her father is 5. _____.

Ⓒ Mary and Takeshi went to a Japanese restaurant. They are looking at the menu a waitress brought. Listen to the dialogue and answer the following questions. 🔊 Disk1-32

1. How much are these items?

　　a. すきやき (¥   )   b. うどん (¥   )   c. てんぷら (¥   )

2. What did Mary order? Why did she decide on it?

3. What did Takeshi order?

第3課 1 Verb Conjugation

▶ Memorize the thirteen verbs introduced in Lesson 3. Read the explanation about verb conjugation and complete the following tables.

Ru-verbs

	dictionary form	present affirmative	present negative
1. get up			
2. see			
3. eat			
4. sleep			

U-verbs

	dictionary form	present affirmative	present negative
5. speak			
6. listen			
7. go			
8. read			
9. drink			
10. return			

Irregular Verbs

	dictionary form	present affirmative	present negative
11. come			
12. do			
13. study			

第3課 2 Noun を verb

▶ Write a ます and ません sentence using two of the nouns in each group and a verb of your choice.

Example:

> Noun： さかな　にく　やさい
>
> affirmative　→　わたしは やさいを たべます。
>
> negative　　→　わたしは にくを たべません。

1. Noun： おさけ　おちゃ　コーヒー

   affirmative　→

   negative　　→

2. Noun： にほんの えいが　アメリカの えいが　フランスの えいが

   affirmative　→

   negative　　→

3. Noun： テニス　サッカー (soccer)　バスケットボール (basketball)

   affirmative　→

   negative　　→

4. Noun： ほん　おんがくの ざっし　スポーツの ざっし

   affirmative　→

   negative　　→

5. Noun： にほんの おんがく　ロック (rock)　にほんごの テープ

   affirmative　→

   negative　　→

第3課 3 Verbs with Places

Ⅰ) Where do the following activities take place? Add the places and appropriate particles to the following sentences.

Example: としょかんで ほんを よみます。

1. _____ べんきょうします。

2. _____ テレビを みます。

3. _____ コーヒーを のみます。

4. _____ いきます。

5. _____ かえります。

Ⅱ) Translate the following sentences into Japanese.

1. Mr. Tanaka will go to school.

2. My friend will come to Japan.

3. Ms. Suzuki listens to the tape in the L.L.

4. I speak Japanese at home.

5. I don't eat lunch at home.

第3課 4 Time References

(I) Time Expressions—Read Grammar 4 (pp. 61-62) on time references, and classify the words below into two groups. If the words are *always* used with に, write に after the words.

1. こんばん＿＿＿ 4. いつ＿＿＿ 7. どようび＿＿＿ 10. まいにち＿＿＿

2. しゅうまつ＿＿＿ 5. きょう＿＿＿ 8. あした＿＿＿ 11. まいばん＿＿＿

3. あさ＿＿＿ 6. いま＿＿＿ 9. じゅういちじ＿＿＿

(II) Your Day—Describe what you do during on a typical day. Include the descriptions of activities listed below. Whenever possible, include place and time expressions. Refer to Grammar 6 (pp. 62-63) on the basic order of phrases.

おきる　　いく　　たべる　　べんきょうする　　かえる　　ねる

1. わたしは まいにち ＿＿＿じに ＿＿＿＿＿＿＿＿＿＿＿ます。

2.

3.

4.

5.

(III) Translate the following sentences into Japanese.

1. I speak Japanese every day.

2. I will not watch TV tonight.

3. Mary does not come to school on Saturdays.

第3課 5 Suggestion Using ～ませんか

Ⅰ Study Dialogue I (p. 54) and translate the following exchange.

メアリー： 1. _____

   (Would you like to see a movie tonight?)

たけし： 2. _____

   (Tonight is not a very good time . . .)

メアリー： 3. _____

   (How about tomorrow?)

たけし： 4. _____

   (Sounds great.)

Ⅱ Imagine you ask someone out. Write the dialogue between you and your friend.

You： 1. _____

Friend： 2. _____

You： 3. _____

Friend： 4. _____

第3課 6 Frequency Adverbs

▶ Translate the following sentences into Japanese.

1. I often go to the library.

   わたしは _____ としょかん _____ _____。

2. Sue often comes to my house.

3. I usually get up at six.

4. Professor Yamashita usually goes to sleep at eleven.

5. I sometimes read Japanese newspapers.

6. Takeshi sometimes drinks coffee at that coffee shop.

7. Mary does not eat much.

第3課 7 聞く練習 (Listening Comprehension)
き　れんしゅう

(A) Listen to the dialogue between Sue and Mary. Where will they be? What will they do? [◀))] Disk2-9

	1. Saturday	2. Sunday
Mary	in ＿＿＿＿＿＿＿＿＿＿＿＿＿＿＿	in ＿＿＿＿＿＿＿＿＿＿＿＿＿＿＿
Sue	in/at ＿＿＿＿＿＿＿＿＿＿＿＿＿	in/at ＿＿＿＿＿＿＿＿＿＿＿＿＿

(B) Listen to the dialogue at an evening meeting at a summer camp. The group leader and the students are discussing the schedule for the next day. Complete the schedule below. [◀))] Disk2-10

1. (　　) 6:00 A.M.
2. (　　) 7:30
3. (　　) 9:00
4. (　　) 12:30 P.M.
5. (　　) 1:30
6. (　　) 3:00
7. (　　) 6:00
8. (　　) 7:30
9. (　　) 11:30

| a. breakfast | b. dinner | c. get up | d. go to bed | e. lunch |
| f. play basketball | g. play tennis | h. study | i. watch a movie | |

Ⓒ Listen to the conversation between Sue and her friend. How often does she do the following things? (a = every day, b = often, c = sometimes, d = not often, e = not at all) 🔊 Disk2-11

1. (　　　) study Japanese

2. (　　　) go to the library

3. (　　　) listen to a Japanese tape

4. (　　　) watch American movies

5. (　　　) watch Japanese movies

6. (　　　) play tennis

7. (　　　) drink coffee

Ⓓ Listen to the dialogue between Mary and a Japanese friend of hers and answer the questions below. 🔊 Disk2-12

1. What time is it?　(　　　)

　　a. Eight　　b. Nine　　c. Ten　　d. Eleven

2. What did the man suggest first?　(　　　)

　　a. Coffee at a coffee shop　　b. Beer at a bar　　c. Coffee at his place　　d. Lunch

3. How did the woman turn down his suggestion? (Mark ○ for all that apply.)

　　a. (　　　) By saying that she needs to go back home

　　b. (　　　) By saying that it is too late

　　c. (　　　) By saying that she needs to study

　　d. (　　　) By saying that she needs to go to sleep early

4. What other suggestions did the man make? (Mark ○ for all that apply.)

　　a. (　　　) Listening to Japanese language tapes together

　　b. (　　　) Practicing Japanese at a coffee shop

　　c. (　　　) Having lunch together the next day

　　d. (　　　) Walking her home

第4課 1 Xがあります/います

Ⅰ Translate the following sentences into Japanese.

1. There is a bus stop over there.

2. There will be no class on Thursday.

3. I do not have a dictionary. (lit., There is not a dictionary.)

4. There's Professor Yamashita over there!

5. I have a child. (lit., There is a child.)

Ⅱ Answer the following questions in Japanese.

1. あした、アルバイトがありますか。

2. いつ日本語のクラスがありますか。

3. 日本に友だちがいますか。

4. 兄弟 (brothers and sisters) がいますか。

おねえさん: older sister
いもうと: younger sister
おにいさん: older brother
おとうと: younger brother

第4課 2 Describing Where Things Are

Ⅰ Draw a picture showing the items mentioned in the passage below, each in correct geometrical relation to the others.

辞書はつくえの上です。時計もつくえの上です。ぼうしは辞書と時計の間です。かばんはつくえの下です。つくえはテレビのそばです。

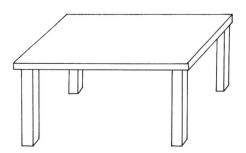

Ⅱ Look at the pictures and answer the following questions.

1. 日本語の本はどこですか。

2. メアリーさんのかさはどこですか。

3. スーさんの辞書はどこですか。

4. 図書館はどこですか。

5. 銀行はどこですか。

(1) Japanese book

(2) Mary's umbrella

(3) Sue's dictionary

(4)(5)

Library

Bank

Post Office

第4課 3 Past Tense (Nouns)

(I) Answer the following questions.

1. きのうは月曜日_{げつようび}でしたか。

2. きのうは十五日_{じゅうごにち}でしたか。

3. 今日_{きょう}の朝_{あさ}ごはんはハンバーガーでしたか。

4. 子供_{こども}の時_{とき}、いい子供_{こども}でしたか。

5. 高校_{こうこう}の時_{とき}、いい学生_{がくせい}でしたか。

(II) Translate the following sentences into Japanese.

1. My bicycle was 30,000 yen.

2. Yesterday was Sunday.

3. Professor Yamada was not a Nihon University student.

クラス _____ なまえ _____

第4課 4 Verb Conjugation (Past Tense)

▶ Fill in the conjugation table below. If you are unclear about the *u*-verb/*ru*-verb distinction, read Grammar 1 in Lesson 3 (pp. 58-59) once again. If you are unclear about the past tense conjugation, refer to the table on p. 79.

U-verbs

	dictionary form	past affirmative	past negative
1. drink			
2. speak			
3. listen			
4. buy			
5. take			
6. write			
7. wait			
8. there is			

Ru-verbs and Irregular Verbs

	dictionary form	past affirmative	past negative
9. eat			
10. get up			
11. do			
12. come			

第4課 5 Past Tense (Verbs)

Ⅰ Read what Takeshi did last weekend and answer the following questions in Japanese.

> Takeshi listened to music at home on Friday.
>
> He worked part-time at a supermarket on Saturday.
>
> He saw a movie with Mary in Kyoto on Sunday.

1. たけしさんは金曜日に手紙を書きましたか。

2. たけしさんは土曜日にどこでアルバイトをしましたか。

3. たけしさんはいつ音楽を聞きましたか。

4. たけしさんは日曜日に何をしましたか。(Fill in the blanks.)

　　たけしさんは_____に_____で

_____と_____を_____。

5. あなたは、週末、何をしましたか。

Ⅱ Translate the following sentences into Japanese.

1. Sue did not take pictures at all.

2. I often ate hamburgers when I was a child.

3. Takeshi did not study much when he was in high school.

第4課 6 も

▶ Translate the sentences into Japanese. Note that the particle も replaces は, が, and を, but goes side by side with other particles.

1. Mary went to Osaka last week. Takeshi went to Osaka last week, too.

2. There is a Japanese class on Monday. There is a history class on Monday, too.

3. There is a bookstore over there. There is a restaurant, too.

4. I bought a dictionary. I bought a magazine, too.

5. I drink tea. I drink coffee, too.

6. Mary will go to Korea (韓国). She will go to China (中国), too.

7. Michiko ate hamburgers on Friday. She ate hamburgers on Saturday, too.

8. Sue bought souvenirs at a temple. She bought souvenirs at a department store, too.

9. I took pictures at school yesterday. I took pictures at home, too.

第4課 7 Word Order and Particles

Ⅰ Translate the following sentences into Japanese.

1. Mary studied Japanese for two hours yesterday.
             (3)   (2)   (1)

    メアリーさんは _____ _____ _____ 。
                  (1)   (2)   (3)

2. Takeshi waited for Mary for one hour in front of the department store.
             (3)   (2)   (1)

    たけしさんは _____ _____ _____ 。
            (1)   (2)   (3)

3. Sue listens to the tape at the Language Lab for about one hour every day.
         (4)   (3)   (2)   (1)

    スーさんは _____ _____ _____
            (1)   (2)   (3)

    _____ 。
        (4)

Ⅱ Fill in the particles that are missing. You may want to refer to the Vocabulary section (pp. 74-75), where the particle that goes with each of the new verbs is shown in parentheses.

1. 私はあした友だち_____会います。

2. メアリーさんは京都のお寺で写真_____撮りました。

3. 私は喫茶店でロバートさん_____待ちました。

4. スーパーで肉_____買いました。

5. 私はフランス語_____わかりません。

6. 私はきのう手紙_____書きませんでした。

第4課 8 聞く練習 (Listening Comprehension)
き　　れんしゅう

Ⓐ Mary is talking with her homestay father. Listen to the dialogue and answer the questions in English. 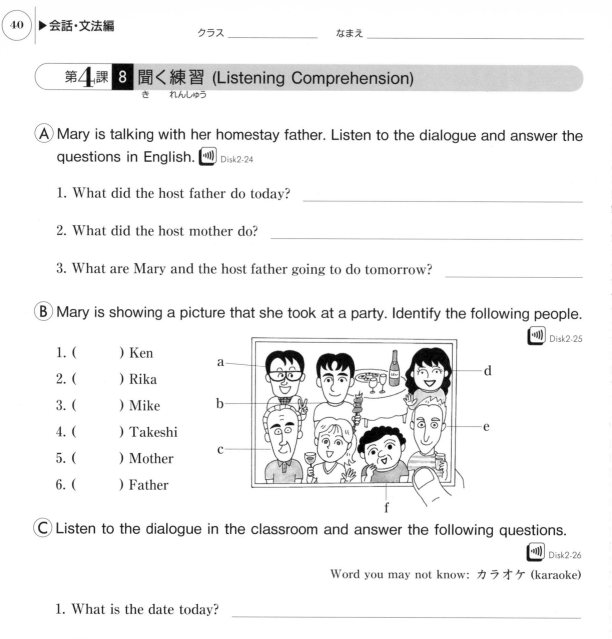 Disk2-24

1. What did the host father do today? _____

2. What did the host mother do? _____

3. What are Mary and the host father going to do tomorrow? _____

Ⓑ Mary is showing a picture that she took at a party. Identify the following people.

Disk2-25

1. (　　　) Ken

2. (　　　) Rika

3. (　　　) Mike

4. (　　　) Takeshi

5. (　　　) Mother

6. (　　　) Father

Ⓒ Listen to the dialogue in the classroom and answer the following questions.

Disk2-26

Word you may not know: カラオケ (karaoke)

1. What is the date today? _____

2. What day is today? _____

3. Who did these things? Mark ○ for the things they did.

	a. studied	b. danced	c. went to Tokyo	d. wrote a letter	e. went to karaoke	f. did shopping
Sue						
Mary						
Robert						

4. Robert will be in trouble. Why? _____

第5課 1 Adjectives (Present Tense)

Ⅰ) For each of the adjectives below, write the meaning and determine whether it is an い- or a な-adjective. (You may want to refer to the Vocabulary section [pp. 98-99].) Then, turn it into the negative, paying attention to the difference between the two types of adjectives.

	meaning	adjective type	negative
Ex. いそがしいです	busy	ⓘ / な	いそがしくありません
1. きらいです		い / な	
2. あたらしいです		い / な	
3. やさしいです		い / な	
4. しずかです		い / な	
5. ハンサムです		い / な	
6. つまらないです		い / な	
7. こわいです		い / な	

Ⅱ) Translate the following sentences into Japanese.

1. This watch is expensive.

2. This coffee is not delicious.

3. Professor Yamashita is energetic.

4. Books are not cheap.

5. I will not be free tomorrow.

クラス _____ なまえ _____

第5課 2 Adjective Conjugation—1

▶ Fill in the conjugation table below.

い-adjectives

	1. large	2. expensive
dictionary form		
present affirmative		
present negative		
past affirmative		
past negative		

	3. frightening	4. interesting
dictionary form		
present affirmative		
present negative		
past affirmative		
past negative		

	5. old	6. good
dictionary form		
present affirmative		
present negative		
past affirmative		
past negative		

第5課 3 Adjective Conjugation—2

▶ Fill in the conjugation table below.

な-adjectives

	1. quiet	2. beautiful
dictionary form		
present affirmative		
present negative		
past affirmative		
past negative		

	3. healthy	4. fond
dictionary form		
present affirmative		
present negative		
past affirmative		
past negative		

	5. disgusted	6. lively
dictionary form		
present affirmative		
present negative		
past affirmative		
past negative		

第5課 4 Adjectives (Past Tense)

(I) Answer the questions.

1. 先週はひまでしたか。
　　せんしゅう

2. テストは難しかったですか。
　　　　　むずか

3. きのうは暑かったですか。
　　　　　あつ

4. 週末は楽しかったですか。
　　しゅうまつ　たの

5. きのうの晩ごはんはおいしかったですか。
　　　　　　ばん

(II) Translate the following sentences into Japanese.

1. I was busy yesterday.

2. The homework was difficult.

3. My room was not clean.

4. The weather was good.

5. The trip was not fun.

6. The tickets were not expensive.

第5課 5 Adjective ＋ Noun

Ⓘ Look at the pictures and answer the questions.

Ex.	1.	2.	3.	4.
small	old	quiet	scary	beautiful

Example:　どんな部屋ですか。　→　小さい部屋です。

1. どんな自転車ですか。

　→

2. どんな町ですか。

　→

3. どんな人ですか。

　→

4. どんな家ですか。

　→

Ⓘ Translate the following sentences.

1. I met a kind person.

2. I bought an inexpensive ticket.

3. I read an interesting book last week.

クラス _____ なまえ _____

第5課 6 好き(な)/きらい(な)

▶ Write down the sentences telling if you like / dislike the things below. Use 好き(な) for "like" and きらい(な) for "don't like." Use 大～ for emphasis.

Example: homework → 私は宿題が大好きです。

1. Japanese class

    →

2. this town

    →

3. Mondays

    →

4. ocean

    →

5. cats

    →

6. cold mornings

    →

7. fish

    →

8. frightening movies

    →

9. (your own sentences)

第5課 7 〜ましょう

（Ⅰ）You and your friend will spend one day together. Complete the underlined parts with ましょう.

友_{とも}だち：どこに行_いきますか。

私_{わたし}：　1. _____

友_{とも}だち：いいですね。そこで何_{なに}をしますか。

私_{わたし}：　2. _____。それから、

　　　　3. _____

友_{とも}だち：何時_{なんじ}に会_あいますか。

私_{わたし}：　4. _____

（Ⅱ）Translate the following sentences into Japanese.

1. Let's take pictures here.

2. Let's watch this movie tonight.

3. Let's wait in the coffee shop.

4. This kanji is difficult. Let's ask our teacher.

5. Let's do the homework together.

第**5**課 **8** 聞く練習 (Listening Comprehension)
き　　れんしゅう

A Listen to the dialogue between a real estate agent and his customer and choose the appropriate answers. ▣ Disk3-11　　Word you may not know: 一か月 (one month)
いっ　げつ

1. The house is [new / old].

2. The house is [clean / not clean].

3. The house is [quiet / not quiet].

4. The rooms are [big / not big].

5. There are [many / not many] rooms.

6. The rent is [90,400 / 94,000] yen a month.

B Listen to the TV game show "Who's My Date?" Three men want to invite Ms. Suzuki on a date. ▣ Disk3-12

Word you may not know: おめでとうございます。 (Congratulations.)

1. Fill in the blanks in English.

	Favorite type	What he does on holidays
a. 吉田 よしだ	＿＿＿＿＿＿＿＿＿＿＿＿	＿＿＿＿＿＿＿＿＿＿＿＿
b. 川口 かわぐち	＿＿＿＿＿＿＿＿＿＿＿＿	＿＿＿＿＿＿＿＿＿＿＿＿
c. 中山 なかやま	＿＿＿＿＿＿＿＿＿＿＿＿	＿＿＿＿＿＿＿＿＿＿＿＿

2. Who did Ms. Suzuki choose? ＿＿＿＿＿＿＿＿＿＿＿

C Listen to the interview with Mary and Takeshi and fill in the chart with the following letters: a = likes, b = doesn't like very much, c = hates. ▣ Disk3-13

	1. Rock	2. Jazz	3. Classical music	4. Suspense movies	5. Horror movies
Mary					——
Takeshi					

第6課 1 Te-form —1

▶ Review Grammar 1 (pp. 118-119) and conjugate the verbs below into their respective *te*-forms. The numbers indicate the lesson in which the verbs first appeared.

Ru-verbs

1. おきる (3)　→

2. たべる (3)　→

3. ねる (3)　→

4. みる (3)　→

5. いる (4)　→

6. でかける (5) →

U-verbs ending with う

7. あう (4)　　→

8. かう (4)　　→

U-verbs ending with く

9. きく (3)　　→

10. かく (4)　　→

U-verbs ending with く (irregular)

11. いく (3)　　→

U-verbs ending with ぐ

12. およぐ (5)　→

U-verbs ending with す

13. はなす (3)　→

U-verbs ending with つ

14. まつ (4)　　→

U-verbs ending with む

15. のむ (3)　　→

16. よむ (3)　　→

U-verbs ending with る

17. かえる (3)　→

18. ある (4)　　→

19. とる (4)　　→

20. わかる (4)　→

21. のる (5)　　→

22. やる (5)　　→

Irregular Verbs

23. くる (3)　　→

24. する (3)　　→

25. べんきょうする (3)　→

クラス _____   なまえ _____

第6課 2 ～てください

I Write what each person says using ～てください.

1. take a picture

2. teach this kanji

3. carry this bag

4. listen to this tape

5. sit down

6. bring a book

1.

2.

3.

4.

5.

6.

II Write three request sentences using ～てください. Indicate in parentheses who you are going to ask to do those things.

1. (   )

2. (   )

3. (   )

第6課 3 *Te*-form ―2

▶ Review the Vocabulary section (pp. 116-117) and the Grammar (pp. 118-119) and fill in the following table.

Ru-verbs

	long form (〜ます)	*te*-form	meaning
1. あける			
2. おしえる			
3. おりる			
4. かりる			
5. しめる			
6. つける			
7. でんわをかける			
8. わすれる			

U-verbs

	long form (〜ます)	*te*-form	meaning
9. たばこをすう			
10. つかう			
11. てつだう			

12. いそぐ			

	long form (〜ます)	*te*-form	meaning
13. かえす			
14. けす			

15. たつ			
16. もつ			

17. しぬ			

18. あそぶ			

19. やすむ			

20. すわる			
21. はいる			

Irregular Verbs

	long form (〜ます)	*te*-form	meaning
22. つれてくる			
23. もってくる			

第6課 4 〜てもいいです／〜てはいけません

(I) Look at the signs and make sentences using 〜てはいけません.

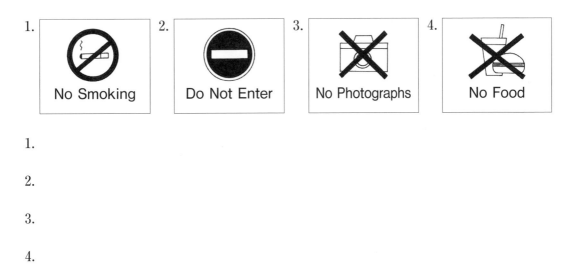

1. No Smoking　2. Do Not Enter　3. No Photographs　4. No Food

1.

2.

3.

4.

(II) Translate the following sentences into Japanese.

1. May I go out tonight?

2. May I turn off the TV?

3. You must not watch this movie alone. You are 16 years old!

4. You must not forget the homework.

5. I am allowed to work part-time (lit., "do" a part-time job) in Japan.

(III) Describe two things that you are allowed to do/prohibited from doing at the place you now live.

1.

2.

第6課 5 Describing Two Activities

Ⅰ The pictures below describe what Takeshi did yesterday. Make sentences using
te-forms.

1.

2.

3.

4.

Ⅱ Translate the following sentences.

1. I will go to the library and return the book tomorrow.

2. Mary and Takeshi met and talked for about an hour.

3. My friend went to China and did not return.

第6課 6 ～から

(Ⅰ) Translate the following sentences, using ～から.

1. I am not free today. (It's) because I have a test tomorrow.

2. The test was not difficult. (That was) because I had studied a lot.

3. Let's go out tonight. (It's) because tomorrow is a holiday.

4. I helped my mother. (It's) because she was busy.

5. I will not drink coffee. (It's) because I drank coffee in the morning.

(Ⅱ) Complete the dialogue below.

A： 1. _____

B： どうしてですか。

A： 2. _____ から。

第6課 7 聞く練習 (Listening Comprehension)
き　　れんしゅう

Ⓐ Listen to the dialogue at a youth hostel. Mark T if the following statements are true. Mark F if not true. 🔊 Disk3-23

1. (　　　　) The breakfast starts at 6:30.

2. (　　　　) Smoking is not permitted in the room.

3. (　　　　) You can take a shower in the morning.

4. (　　　　) There is no coin laundry here.

Ⓑ Your roommate has gone away for a week. She has left a message on your answering machine. Listen to it and mark ○ for what you are asked to do.

🔊 Disk3-24

Word you may not know: れいぞうこ (refrigerator)

You are asked to:

1. (　　　　) open the window

2. (　　　　) water the plants

3. (　　　　) drink leftover milk

4. (　　　　) return a book to Mary

5. (　　　　) borrow a camera from Robert

6. (　　　　) do some shopping for a party

Ⓒ Takeshi is trying to organize a picnic. Listen to the dialogue and answer the questions in English. 🔊 Disk3-25

1. When is NOT convenient for each of them? Why?

	a. Inconvenient day	b. Reasons
Michiko		
Sue		
Robert		

2. When did they decide to go on the picnic? _____

第7課 1 *Te*-form

▶ Decide whether they are *u-*, *ru-*, or irregular verbs and fill in the table below.

	u/ru/ irregular	long form	*te*-form
Ex. ある	*u*	あります	あって
1. わかる			
2. やる			
3. けす			
4. たつ			
5. おきる			
6. かえる			
7. くる			
8. する			
9. あそぶ			
10. かける			
11. きる			
12. かぶる			
13. つとめる			
14. はく			
15. うたう			
16. すむ			
17. けっこんする			

第7課 2 ～ている (Actions in Progress)

Ⅰ Describe the following pictures, using ～ています.

1.　2.　3.　4.　5.

1.

2.

3.

4.

5.

Ⅱ Answer the following questions in Japanese.

1. 今、何をしていますか。
   いま　なに

2. きのうの午後八時ごろ何をしていましたか。
   ご　ご　はち　じ　　　　なに

Ⅲ Translate the following sentences.

1. Mary is waiting for a bus at the bus stop.

2. At two o'clock yesterday, Takeshi was playing tennis with a friend.

3. I called home. My big sister was doing her homework.

第7課 3 〜ている (Result of a Change)

I This is Michiko's family. Answer the following questions in Japanese.

Father	51 years old	works for a bank	lives in Nagano
Mother	47 years old	works for a hospital	lives in Nagano
Older sister	23 years old	college student; married	lives in Tokyo
Younger brother	16 years old	student	lives in Nagano

1. お父さんは何をしていますか。

2. お母さんは何をしていますか。

3. お姉さんは勤めていますか。

4. お姉さんは結婚していますか。

5. お姉さんは長野に住んでいますか。

6. 弟さんはどこに住んでいますか。

7. お父さんは何歳ですか。

II Write about your family. Try to use expressions you have learned in this lesson.

第7課 4 Describing People

Ⅰ Translate the following sentences.

1. Yasuo wears glasses.

2. Noriko is wearing a new T-shirt today.

3. Noriko is skinny, but Yasuo is overweight.

4. Michiko has short hair.

5. Michiko is not tall.

6. Michiko is very bright.

Ⅱ You are an eyewitness testifying in court. Describe the person you saw at the scene of the crime.

1. Height:

2. Hair:

3. Glasses:

4. Eyes:

5. Clothes (above the waistline):

6. Clothes (below the waistline):

7. Shoes:

8. What he was doing at the time:

第7課 5 *Te*-forms for Joining Sentences

Ⓘ Look at the following pictures and complete the sentences.

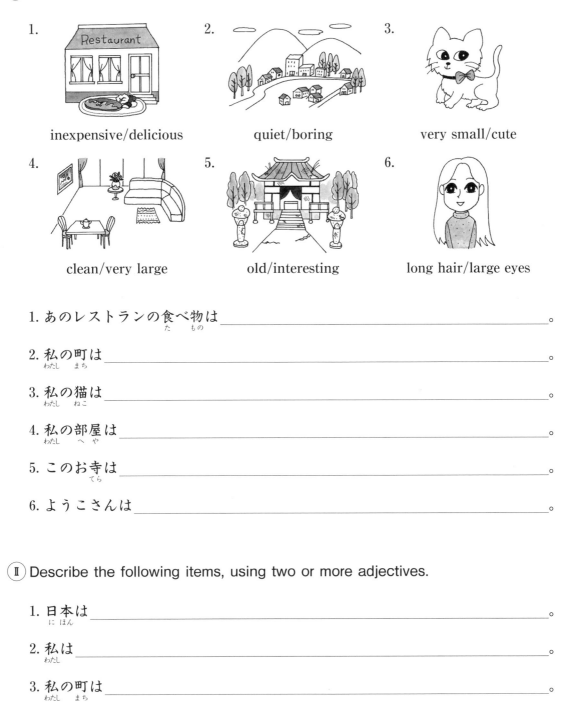

1. inexpensive/delicious

2. quiet/boring

3. very small/cute

4. clean/very large

5. old/interesting

6. long hair/large eyes

1. あのレストランの食べ物は _____。

2. 私の町は _____。

3. 私の猫は _____。

4. 私の部屋は _____。

5. このお寺は _____。

6. ようこさんは _____。

Ⓘ Describe the following items, using two or more adjectives.

1. 日本は _____。

2. 私は _____。

3. 私の町は _____。

4. 私の友だちは _____。

第7課 6 Verb stem ＋ に 行く/来る/帰る
(い)(く)(かえ)

Ⅰ Rewrite the sentences below, using the verb stem ＋ に行く/来る/帰る pattern.
(い)(く)(かえ)

Example:　図書館に行って、本を借ります。　→　図書館に本を借りに行きます。
　　　　　(と しょかん)(い)　　(ほん)(か)　　　　　　(と しょかん)(ほん)(か)(い)

1. 大阪に行って、友だちに会います。
(おおさか)(い)　　(とも)　　(あ)

　　→

2. 家に帰って、晩ごはんを食べます。
(いえ)(かえ)　　(ばん)　　　(た)

　　→

3. きのう、町に行って、雑誌を買いました。
　　　　(まち)(い)　　(ざっし)(か)

　　→

4. 私は 週末京都に行って、写真を撮りました。
(わたし)　(しゅうまつきょう と)(い)　　(しゃしん)(と)

　　→

5. ロバートさんは よく私のアパートに来て、テレビを見ます。
　　　　　　　　　(わたし)　　　　　(き)　　　　　(み)

　　→

Ⅱ Make your own sentences, using a place from the list below.

(Ex.) 大学 (だいがく)	日本 (にほん)	食堂 (しょくどう)	喫茶店 (きっさ てん)	友だちのうち (とも)	図書館 (と しょかん)	お寺 (てら)	海 (うみ)

Example:　大学　→　大学に友だちに会いに行きます。
　　　　　(だいがく)　　(だいがく)(とも)(あ)(い)

1.

2.

3.

4.

第7課 7 Counting People

▶ Answer the questions in Japanese.

1. 日本語のクラスに女の人が何人いますか。

2. 日本語のクラスに男の人が何人いますか。

3. 兄弟がいますか。何人いますか。

4. ルームメート (roommate) がいますか。何人いますか。

5. あなたの大学に学生が何人いますか。

6. あなたの町に人が何人住んでいますか。

第7課 8 聞く練習 (Listening Comprehension)
き　　れんしゅう

A One student was assaulted by someone at the dorm. A police officer is asking Robert what he and the other students were doing at the time of the incident. Write down in English what each student was doing. 🔊 Disk4-9

Word you may not know: ほかの (other)

1. Robert: ＿＿＿＿＿＿＿＿＿＿＿＿＿＿＿＿＿＿＿＿＿＿＿＿＿＿＿＿＿＿＿

2. Sue: ＿＿＿＿＿＿＿＿＿＿＿＿＿＿＿＿＿＿＿＿＿＿＿＿＿＿＿＿＿＿＿

3. Takeshi: ＿＿＿＿＿＿＿＿＿＿＿＿＿＿＿＿＿＿＿＿＿＿＿＿＿＿＿＿＿＿＿

4. Ken: ＿＿＿＿＿＿＿＿＿＿＿＿＿＿＿＿＿＿＿＿＿＿＿＿＿＿＿＿＿＿＿

5. Michiko: ＿＿＿＿＿＿＿＿＿＿＿＿＿＿＿＿＿＿＿＿＿＿＿＿＿＿＿＿＿＿＿

6. Tom: ＿＿＿＿＿＿＿＿＿＿＿＿＿＿＿＿＿＿＿＿＿＿＿＿＿＿＿＿＿＿＿

B Listen to a TV reporter at a celebrity's party. Choose appropriate descriptions for each celebrity. 🔊 Disk4-10

1. Arnold Stallone ( ) ( )
2. Noguchi Hiroko ( ) ( )
3. Matsumoto Seiko ( ) ( )
4. Matsumoto Seiko's new boyfriend ( ) ( )

| a. wears jeans | b. wears a hat | c. wears glasses | d. has short hair |
| e. has long hair | f. is cute | g. is fat | h. is tall |

C Mary is interviewing people who are walking downtown on Sunday. What is each interviewee doing today? Choose the appropriate answers. 🔊 Disk4-11

1. Tanaka: a. buying flowers b. buying cards c. buying a CD
2. Sato: a. playing games b. singing songs c. playing sports
3. Suzuki: a. working at a department store b. seeing his younger sister

c. talking with his younger brother

第8課 1 Short Forms (Present Tense)

▶ Fill in the conjugation table below. Note that *ru*-verbs, *u*-verbs, and irregular verbs appear randomly on this sheet.

	dictionary form	short, negative	long, affirmative	*te*-form
Ex. eat	たべる	たべない	たべます	たべて
1. open				
2. buy				
3. sit down				
4. come				
5. die				
6. turn off				
7. study				
8. write				
9. there is				
10. drink				
11. understand				
12. wait				
13. play				
14. hurry				

第8課 2 Short Forms (Informal Speech)

Ⅰ Make informal question sentences using the cues and answer them in the negative.

Example: (Do you) study today? → Q：今日、勉強する？　A：ううん、しない。

1. (Do you) often ride a bus?

→　Q：　　　　　　　　　　　　　A：

2. (Do you) speak Japanese every day?

→　Q：　　　　　　　　　　　　　A：

3. (Do you) have homework today?

→　Q：　　　　　　　　　　　　　A：

4. (Will you) go out this weekend?

→　Q：　　　　　　　　　　　　　A：

5. Are you free tomorrow?

→　Q：　　　　　　　　　　　　　A：

6. Are you Japanese?

→　Q：　　　　　　　　　　　　　A：

7. Is it hot?

→　Q：　　　　　　　　　　　　　A：

Ⅱ Answer the following questions in informal speech.

1. 今日は何曜日？

2. どんな食べ物がきらい？

3. 今週の週末、何をする？

第8課 3 Quotations (〜と思います)

(I) Translate the following sentences. In sentences 5-8, "I don't think . . ." should be translated as 〜ないと思います.

1. I think food is expensive in Japan.

2. I think Professor Yamashita is handsome.

3. I think this woman is Mary's Japanese teacher.

4. I think Professor Yamashita reads many books.

5. I don't think this town is interesting. (lit., I think this town is not interesting.)

6. I don't think Saeko drinks sake.

7. I don't think Chieko likes Mayumi.

8. I don't think Noriko will come to school today.

(II) Answer the following questions, using 〜と思います.

1. あしたはどんな天気ですか。

2. 来週は忙しいですか。

3. あなたの日本語の先生は、料理が上手ですか。

4. あなたの日本語の先生は、今週の週末、何をしますか。

第8課 4 Quotations (〜と言っていました)

▶ Ask someone (preferably Japanese) the following questions. Report the answers using 〜と言っていました.

Example: 大学生ですか。 → 田中さんは大学生だと言っていました。

1. 毎日、楽しいですか。

→

2. どんな料理が好きですか。

→

3. お酒を飲みますか。

→

4. どんなスポーツをよくしますか。

→

5. 兄弟がいますか。

→

6. どこに住んでいますか。

→

7. 結婚していますか。

→

8. 車を持っていますか。

→

9. 週末はたいてい何をしますか。

→

10. (your own question)

→

Get the signature of the person you interviewed: ＿＿＿＿＿＿＿＿＿＿＿＿＿＿

第8課 5 〜ないでください

Ⅰ Translate the following sentences.

Example: Please don't wait for me. (Because) I will be late.

→ 私を待たないでください。遅くなりますから。

1. Please don't forget your umbrella. (Because) It will rain this afternoon.

→

2. Please don't open the window. (Because) I am cold.

→

3. Please don't turn off the TV. (Because) I'm watching the news (ニュース).

→

4. Please don't read that letter. (Because) It is my letter.

→

Ⅱ Write the dictionary form of each of the verbs used in the following sentences.

1. きらないでください。 _____

2. きないでください。 _____

3. こないでください。 _____

4. かけないでください。 _____

5. かかないでください。 _____

6. しないでください。 _____

7. しなないでください。 _____

8. かえらないでください。 _____

9. かわないでください。 _____

クラス _____ なまえ _____

第8課 6 Verb のが好きです
す

Ⅰ Write what you are good at/what you are not good at/what you like to do/what you don't like to do, using the verbs in the box.

speaking Japanese	driving a car	taking pictures	singing
listening to a tape	taking a bath	playing sports	cooking
doing laundry	cleaning	washing a car	

1. 私は_____下手です。
   わたし　　　　　　　　　　　　　　　　　　　　　　　　　へ　た

2. 私はあまり_____上手じゃありません。
   わたし　　　　　　　　　　　　　　　　　　　　　　　じょう ず

3. 私は_____大好きです。
   わたし　　　　　　　　　　　　　　　　　　　　　　　だい す

4. 私は_____きらいです。
   わたし

5. 私はあまり_____好きじゃありません。
   わたし　　　　　　　　　　　　　　　　　　　　　　　す

Ⅱ Translate the following sentences.

1. Erika is very good at making friends.

2. Kiyoshi loves reading books.

3. Makoto hates cleaning the room.

4. Yoshie is not good at driving a car.

5. Yuki doesn't like doing laundry very much.

第8課 7 が・何か and 何も
なに   なに

(I) Look at the picture at a party and complete the following conversations.

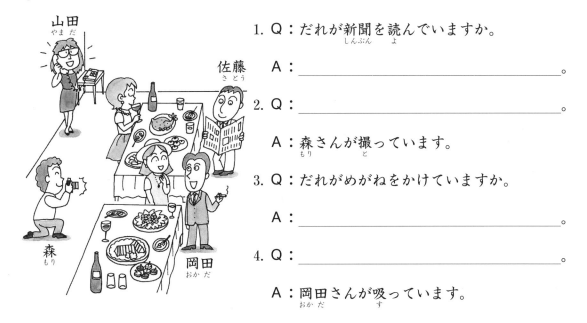

山田
やまだ

佐藤
さとう

森
もり

岡田
おかだ

1. Q：だれが新聞を読んでいますか。
　　　　　　しんぶん　よ

　　A：_____。

2. Q：_____。

　　A：森さんが撮っています。
　　　　もり　　　と

3. Q：だれがめがねをかけていますか。

　　A：_____。

4. Q：_____。

　　A：岡田さんが吸っています。
　　　　おかだ　　　す

(II) Translate the following sentences. (Note especially that 何か and 何も are
なに　　　　　なに
normally not accompanied by particles.)

1. Q：Did you eat anything this morning?

　　A：No, I did not eat anything this morning.

2. Q：What will you do over the weekend?

　　A：I won't do anything.

3. Yoshio said something, but I did not understand.

4. Would you like to drink anything?

クラス＿＿＿＿＿＿＿＿　　なまえ＿＿＿＿＿＿＿＿＿＿＿＿＿＿＿＿

第8課 8 聞く練習 (Listening Comprehension)
き　　れんしゅう

(A) Listen to the CD and choose the picture that describes the situation in which you are likely to hear each of the sentences. 📢 Disk4-23

1. (　　)　2. (　　)　3. (　　)　4. (　　)　5. (　　)　6. (　　)　7. (　　)

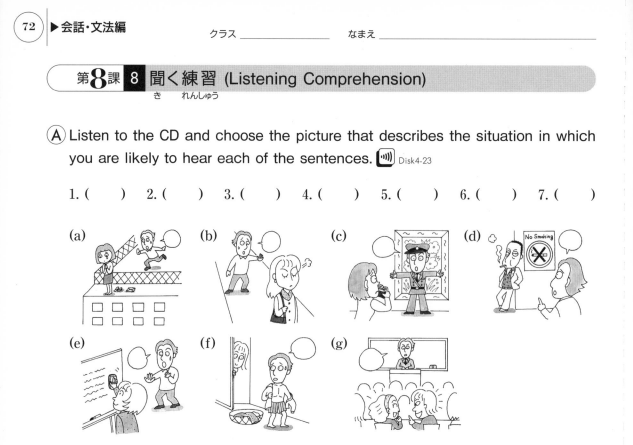

(a)　　　　　(b)　　　　　(c)　　　　　(d)

(e)　　　　　(f)　　　　　(g)

(B) Robert and Ken are talking. Listen to the dialogue and answer the questions.

📢 Disk4-24

1. When are they going to play basketball?　＿＿＿＿＿＿＿＿＿＿＿＿＿＿＿＿＿

2. Is Takeshi coming to play? Why? Why not?　＿＿＿＿＿＿＿＿＿＿＿＿＿＿＿＿＿

3. Is Tom coming also? Why? Why not?　＿＿＿＿＿＿＿＿＿＿＿＿＿＿＿＿＿

(C) Mary is reporting her interview with Professor Honma to the class. Circle every item that is true according to Mary's interview. 📢 Disk4-25

1. Prof. Honma likes a woman who is:

    [a. pretty　　b. tall　　c. short　　d. gentle　　e. smart　　f. slim].

2. He spends his weekends:

    [a. playing baseball　　b. playing tennis　　c. watching sports games　　d. dating].

3. His students in a Japanese class are:

    [a. lively　　b. quiet　　c. diligent　　d. kind].

第9課 1 Past Tense Short Forms

▶ Complete the chart below.

Verb

dictionary form	past, affirmative	past, negative	long, present
Ex. たべる	たべた	たべなかった	たべます
1. よむ			
2. あそぶ			
3. おぼえる			
4. いく			
5. もらう			
6. おどる			
7. およぐ			
8. ひく			
9. やすむ			
10. する			
11. くる			

Adjective/Noun

dictionary form	past, affirmative	past, negative
Ex. おもしろい	おもしろかった	おもしろくなかった
12. わかい		
13. かっこいい		
Ex. いじわる (な)	いじわるだった	いじわるじゃなかった
14. きれい (な)		
15. にちようび		

第9課 2 Past Tense Short Forms (Informal Speech)

Ⅰ Make informal question sentences using the cues and answer them in the negative.

Example: きのう、勉強する
→ Q：きのう、勉強した？ A：ううん、しなかった。

1. きのう、友だちに会う
→ Q：　　　　　　　　　A：

2. きのう、運動する
→ Q：　　　　　　　　　A：

3. 先週、試験がある
→ Q：　　　　　　　　　A：

4. 先週の週末、大学に来る
→ Q：　　　　　　　　　A：

5. 先週の週末、楽しい
→ Q：　　　　　　　　　A：

6. 子供の時、髪が長い
→ Q：　　　　　　　　　A：

7. 子供の時、勉強がきらい
→ Q：　　　　　　　　　A：

Ⅱ Make your own questions you want to ask your friend about his/her childhood in informal speech.

Example: 子供の時、よくスポーツをした？

1.

2.

3.

第9課 3 Past Tense Short Forms (〜と思います)
おも

▶ Translate the following sentences, using the short form ＋ と思います. In sentences 6-10, "I don't think . . ." should be translated as 〜なかったと思います.
おも

1. I think Yoshiko was good at skiing when she was a child.

2. I think Tadashi's younger brother was good-looking when he was young.

3. I think the concert began at 9 o'clock.

4. I think this song was popular when I was a child.

5. I think Saeko did physical exercises last weekend.

6. I don't think the last week's exam was difficult. (lit., I think the last week's exam was not difficult.)

7. I don't think Professor Yamashita was sick yesterday.

8. I don't think Mie was mean when she was a child.

9. I don't think Masako received a letter from Mari.

クラス _____ なまえ _____

第9課 4 Quotations (〜と言っていました)

▶ Ask someone (preferably Japanese) the following questions. Report the answers using 〜と言っていました.

Example: 仕事は何ですか。 → 田中さんは会社員だと言っていました。

1. どんな音楽をよく聞きますか。

　→

2. 何をするのがきらいですか。

　→

3. 先週の週末、何をしましたか。

　→

4. 子供の時、いい子でしたか。

　→

5. 子供の時、背が高かったですか。

　→

6. 子供の時、学校が好きでしたか。

　→

7. 子供の時、どこに住んでいましたか。

　→

8. 子供の時、よく何をしましたか。

　→

9. (your own question)

　→

Get the signature of the person you interviewed: _____

第9課 5 Qualifying Nouns with Verbs

▶ Look at the picture, and answer the questions. Use the pattern ○○さんは～ている人(ひと)です, describing what each person is currently doing.

1. みどりさんはどの人(ひと)ですか。

2. けんいちさんはどの人(ひと)ですか。

3. ともこさんはどの人(ひと)ですか。

4. しんじさんはどの人(ひと)ですか。

5. えりかさんはどの人(ひと)ですか。

第9課 6 まだ〜ていません

▶ Translate the following sentences. Note that answers to もう questions require different verb forms in the affirmative and in the negative. If you are unclear, review Grammar 3 (pp. 176-177).

1. Q：Have you eaten lunch yet?

   A：No, I haven't eaten yet.

2. Q：Have you been to Tokyo yet? (Use 行く.)

   A：Yes, I have (been there) already.

3. Q：Have you bought a kanji dictionary yet?

   A：No I haven't bought (one) yet.

4. Q：Have you talked with the new teacher yet?

   A：No, I haven't talked (with her) yet.

5. Q：Have you done the homework yet?

   A：Yes, I have (done it) already.

第9課 7 ～から

(I) Translate the following sentences.

1. I won't do physical exercises because I am sick today.

2. Today's exam was easy because I memorized all the vocabulary.

3. Masako is very popular because she is good at dancing.

4. I was very lonely because I did not have any friends.

5. I went to see Kabuki with a friend because I received two tickets.

(II) Answer the questions, using the short form ＋ から.

Example:　Ｑ：きのう勉強しましたか。
　　　　　Ａ：いいえ、宿題がなかったから、勉強しませんでした。

1. Ｑ：先週は忙しかったですか。

　　Ａ：＿＿＿＿＿＿＿＿＿＿＿＿＿＿＿＿＿＿＿＿＿＿＿＿＿＿＿＿＿。

2. Ｑ：きのう、学校に来ましたか。

　　Ａ：＿＿＿＿＿＿＿＿＿＿＿＿＿＿＿＿＿＿＿＿＿＿＿＿＿＿＿＿＿。

3. Ｑ：今週の週末、出かけますか。

　　Ａ：＿＿＿＿＿＿＿＿＿＿＿＿＿＿＿＿＿＿＿＿＿＿＿＿＿＿＿＿＿。

4. Ｑ：来年も日本語を勉強しますか。

　　Ａ：＿＿＿＿＿＿＿＿＿＿＿＿＿＿＿＿＿＿＿＿＿＿＿＿＿＿＿＿＿。

第9課 8 聞く練習 (Listening Comprehension)
き　　れんしゅう

(A) Ken and Michiko are taiking. Listen to the dialogue and answer the questions. 🔊 Disk5-9

1. Who waited for whom? _____

2. How long did he/she wait? _____

3. What are they going to do? _____

4. Where is the restaurant located? _____

(B) Jun is showing the picture taken at his birthday party. Where are the following people in the picture? 🔊 Disk5-10

1. (　　　) Jun

2. (　　　) Jun's girlfriend

3. (　　　) Jun's younger sister

4. (　　　) Jun's older sister

5. (　　　) Jun's younger brother

6. (　　　) Jun's father

7. (　　　) Pochi

(C) Listen to the dialogue at a shop. How many of each item did the shopkeeper sell? 🔊 Disk5-11

	How many?	Total amount
1. coffee	_____	¥ _____
2. orange	_____	¥ _____
3. rice ball (おにぎり)	_____	¥ _____
4. tea	_____	¥ _____
5. boxed lunch	_____	¥ _____

第10課 1 Comparison Between Two Items

Ⅰ Translate the following sentences.

1. Tokyo is larger than Osaka.

2. Sundays are more fun than Mondays.

3. Spock (スポック) is smarter than Kirk (カーク).

4. Q：Soccer and baseball, which do you like better?

   A：I like baseball better.

Ⅱ Make comparative sentences (both questions and answers).

Example:　Q：日本語のクラスとビジネスのクラスとどっちのほうが大変ですか。
　　　　　A：日本語のクラスのほうがビジネスのクラスより大変です。

1. Q：

   A：

2. Q：

   A：

3. Q：

   A：

第10課 2 Comparison Among Three or More Items

Ⓘ Using the following categories, make "what/where/who is the most . . ." questions and answer them.

(Ex.)					
日本料理 にほんりょうり	世界の町 せかい　まち	有名人 ゆうめいじん	季節 きせつ	野菜 やさい	外国語 がいこくご

Example:

Q：日本料理の中で、何がいちばんおいしいですか。
　　にほんりょうり　なか　なに

A：すしがいちばんおいしいです。／すしがいちばんおいしいと思います。
　　　　　　　　　　　　　　　　　　　　　　　　　　　　　　　　　　　　おも

1. Q：

　　A：

2. Q：

　　A：

3. Q：

　　A：

Ⅱ Translate the following sentences.

1. Q：Between Chinese, Korean, and Japanese, which is the most difficult?

　　A：The Korean language is the most difficult.

2. Q：Between meat, fish, and vegetables, which do you like best?

　　A：(your own answer)

第10課 3 Adjective/noun ＋ の

Ⅰ Look at the pictures and complete the dialogue, using の.

Mary's　　Takeshi's　　Mary's　　Takeshi's

1. Q：メアリーさんのシャツはどちらですか。

   A：＿＿＿＿＿＿＿＿＿＿＿＿＿＿＿＿＿＿＿＿＿＿＿＿＿＿＿＿＿＿。

2. Q：この黒いシャツは＿＿＿＿＿＿＿＿＿＿＿＿＿＿＿＿＿＿＿＿＿＿＿＿。

   A：たけしさんのです。

3. Q：メアリーさんのパンツはどちらですか。

   A：＿＿＿＿＿＿＿＿＿＿＿＿＿＿＿＿＿＿＿＿＿＿＿＿＿＿＿＿＿＿。

4. Q：この長いパンツはスーさんのですか。

   A：＿＿＿＿＿＿＿＿＿＿＿＿＿＿＿＿＿＿＿＿＿＿＿＿＿＿＿＿＿＿。

Ⅱ Translate the following sentences.

1. This clock is expensive. Give me a cheap one.

2. My computer is slower than yours.

3. What kind of movies do you like? ── I like scary ones.

4. This dictionary is old. I will buy a new one.

5. This red sweater is more expensive than that white one.

第10課 4 〜つもりだ

(I) Translate the following sentences, using 〜つもりです.

1. I am planning on going to see a movie this afternoon.

2. I intend to not go out this evening.

3. I intend to work for a Japanese company.

4. I intend to not get married.

5. Because we have an exam next week, I am planning on studying this week.

(II) Answer the following questions using, 〜つもりです.

1. 今晩何をしますか。
　こんばんなに

2. この週末何をしますか。
　　しゅうまつなに

3. 来学期も日本語を勉強しますか。
　らいがっき　にほんご　べんきょう

4. 夏休み／冬休みに何をしますか。
　なつやす　ふゆやす　なに

第10課 5 Adjective ＋ なる

Ⅰ Describe the following changes, using ～なりました.

1.   2.   3.

tall

1.

2.

3.

Ⅱ Translate the following sentences, using the verb なります. Pay attention to the order of elements in the sentences: "(reason clause) から, (main clause)."

1. My room became clean, because I cleaned it this morning.

2. I have become sleepy, because I did not sleep much last night.

3. I have become very good at speaking Japanese, because I practiced a lot.

4. I will be (become) a teacher, because I like children.

第10課 6 ～で行きます/かかります
い

Ⅰ Describe how Mary and her host father commute to school, and how long it takes or how much it costs.

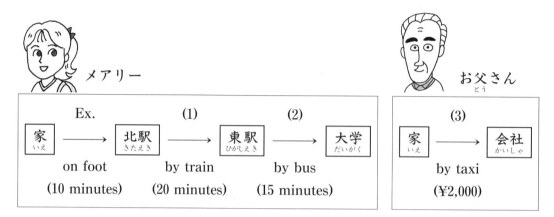

Example: メアリーさんは家から北駅まで歩いて行きます。十分かかります。
いえ　きたえき　ある　い　　じゅっぷん

1.

2.

3.

Ⅱ Answer the following questions.

あなたはどうやって学校に行きますか。どのぐらいかかりますか。
がっこう　い

第10課 7 聞く練習 (Listening Comprehension)
き　れんしゅう

Ⓐ Mary and her friends are talking about the upcoming winter vacation. Listen to the dialogue and fill in the chart in English. 🔊 Disk5-21

	1. Where	2. What to do	3. How long
Mary			
Robert			
Takeshi			
Sue			

Ⓑ Naomi, who is a student at a Japanese language school, wants to go to college in Japan. She is interested in three schools (Hanaoka, Tozai, and Tsushima). Listen to the conversation between Naomi and her Japanese teacher and answer the following questions in English. 🔊 Disk5-22

Word you may not know: 学費 (tuition)
がくひ

1. Which university is the biggest?

2. How much is the tuition at Tsushima University per year?

3. How far is Tozai University from here? How can you get there?

4. Which university has the best Japanese class? Why?

Ⓒ Read Michiko's diary. Listen to the questions on the CD and write your answers in Japanese. 🔊 Disk5-23

> 冬休みに友だちと東京へ行った。12月11日にバスで行った。
> 東京で買い物をした。それから、東京ディズニーランドに
> 行った。12月15日に帰った。とても楽しかった。

1.

2.

3.

4.

5.

第11課 1 ～たい

I Choose from the list below two things you want to do and two things you don't want to do and make sentences.

山に登る　　学校をやめる　　ピアノを習う　　テレビを見る　　働く
やま　のぼ　　がっこう　　　　　　　　なら　　　　　　　　み　　　　　はたら

うそをつく　　友だちとけんかする　　外国に住む　　運動する
　　　　　　　とも　　　　　　　　　がいこく　す　　　うんどう

---

1. What you want to do:

　a.

　b.

2. What you don't want to do:

　a.

　b.

II Translate the following sentences into Japanese.

1. I want to drive a car.

2. I don't want to ride a train.

3. I wanted to own a dog when I was a child.

4. I didn't want to go to school when I was a child.

III Answer the questions.

1. 子供の時、何になりたかったですか。
　こども　とき　なに

2. 子供の時、何がしたくありませんでしたか。
　こども　とき　なに

第11課 2 ～たり～たりする

Ⅰ Translate the following sentences, using ～たり～たり.

1. I watched a movie, shopped, etc., on the weekend.

2. I'll do laundry, study, etc., tomorrow.

3. I met a friend, read a book, etc., yesterday.

4. I practice Japanese, listen to Japanese tapes, etc., in the language lab.

5. I want to climb a mountain, go to a hot spring, etc., this weekend.

6. You must not smoke, drink beer, etc., in class.

Ⅱ Answer the questions, using ～たり～たり.

1. デートの時、何をしますか。
   とき　なに

2. 休みに何をしましたか。
   やす　　なに

3. 子供の時、よく何をしましたか。
   こども　とき　　　なに

4. 今度の週末、何がしたいですか。
   こんど　しゅうまつ　なに

第12課 3 〜ほうがいいです

Ⅰ Translate the following sentences.

1. You had better go to a hospital.

2. You had better memorize kanji.

3. You had better write a letter to your mother.

4. You had better not worry.

5. You had better not smoke.

6. You had better not tell a lie.

Ⅱ Give advice, using 〜ほうがいいですよ.

1. Your friend：あしたテストがあるんです。

   You： _____ 。

2. Your friend：おなかがすいたんです。

   You： _____ 。

3. Your friend: かぜをひいたんです。

   You： _____ 。

第12課 4 〜ので

Ⅰ Translate the following sentences, using 〜ので.

1. I will not go to a party, because I am busy.

2. I came to Japan, because I wanted to study Japanese.

3. I like her, because she is kind.

4. I often go to see movies, because I am interested in foreign countries.

5. My grade was bad, because I didn't study.

6. I will not go to the party tomorrow, because I have a scheduling conflict.

Ⅱ Answer the questions, using 〜ので.

Example: Q：きのう勉強しましたか。
A：いいえ、宿題がなかったので、勉強しませんでした。

1. Q：歌手の中でだれが好きですか。
A：＿＿＿＿＿＿＿＿＿＿＿＿＿＿＿＿＿＿＿＿＿＿＿＿＿＿

2. Q：今いちばんどこに行きたいですか。
A：＿＿＿＿＿＿＿＿＿＿＿＿＿＿＿＿＿＿＿＿＿＿＿＿＿＿

3. Q：将来どんな仕事がしたいですか。
A：＿＿＿＿＿＿＿＿＿＿＿＿＿＿＿＿＿＿＿＿＿＿＿＿＿＿

第12課 5 ～なくちゃいけません

Ⅰ Read the first half of the sentences. Then, choose what you have to do from the list and complete the sentences using ～なくちゃいけません. You may use the same words only once.

| quit the part-time job   buy the textbook   do laundry   practice   get up early |

1. あしたは九時からクラスがあるので、_____。
   く じ

2. 新しいクラスが始まるので、_____。
   あたら   はじ

3. 来週テニスの試合があるので、_____。
   らいしゅう   し あい

4. お母さんが病気なので、_____。
   か あ   びょう き

5. 勉強が忙しくなったので、_____。
   べんきょう   いそが

Ⅱ Write two things you have to do this week and two things you had to do yesterday.

1. This week:

   a.

   b.

2. Yesterday:

   a.

   b.

クラス _____ なまえ _____

第12課 6 ～でしょう

▶You are a meteorologist. Look at the table and report the weather and the temperature of each location with ～でしょう.

Tomorrow's Weather

	天気 てんき	気温 きおん
Ex. 北海道 ほっかいどう		5℃
1. 東京 とうきょう		17℃
2. 大阪 おおさか		20℃
3. 沖縄 おきなわ		24℃

Example: 北海道はあした雪でしょう。
ほっかいどう　　　　ゆき
気温は五度ぐらいでしょう。
きおん　ごど

1.

2.

3.

第12課 7 聞く練習 (Listening Comprehension)
き　　れんしゅう

(A) Listen to the three dialogues at the health clinic. Mark ◯ for the symptoms each patient has and write down the doctor's suggestion in English. [🔊] Disk6-19

Words you may not know: くち (mouth)　さしみ (raw fish)
ねつをはかる (take one's temperature)

Patient	a. sore throat	b. head-ache	c. stomach-ache	d. cough	e. fever	doctor's suggestion
1						
2						
3						

(B) Two colleagues are talking at the office. Listen to the dialogue and answer the following questions in English. [🔊] Disk6-20

1. Are they going out tonight? Why (not)?

2. What does the woman suggest the man should do?

(C) Listen to tomorrow's weather forecast and fill in the chart in English. [🔊] Disk6-21

	Weather	Temperature
1. Tokyo		℃
2. Moscow		℃
3. Bangkok		℃
4. Canberra		℃

読み書き編
よ　か　へん

第1課 1 Hiragana (あ - こ)
だい いっ か

(I) Practice writing the following ten *hiragana* (あ through こ).

a	あ	ー あ / ナ あ	あ	あ	あ					
i	い	し い / い	い	い	い					
u	う	` う / う	う	う	う					
e	え	` え / え	え	え	え					
o	お	ー お / わ お	お	お	お					
ka	か	つ か / カ か	か	か	か					
ki	き	ー き / こ き	き	き	き					
ku	く	く	く	く	く					
ke	け	し け / に け	け	け	け					
ko	こ	ー こ / こ	こ	こ						

(II) Copy and romanize the words below.

1. あおい
(blue)

2. うえ
(above)

3. おか
(hill)

4. あき
(autumn)

5. いけ
(pond)

6. こく
(densely)

(III) Write the words below in *hiragana*.

1. *ou*
(indebted)

2. *ie*
(house)

3. *ai*
(love)

4. *kako*
(past)

5. *kui*
(regret)

6. *eki*
(station)

クラス ＿＿＿＿＿＿＿＿＿＿ なまえ ＿＿＿＿＿＿＿＿＿＿＿＿＿＿＿＿＿＿
(Class) (Name)

第1課 2 Hiragana (さ - と)
だい いっ か

Ⅰ Practice writing the following ten *hiragana* (さ through と).

Ⅱ Copy and romanize the words below.

1. あした
   (tomorrow)

2. とち
   (land)

3. かたて
   (one hand)

4. おさけ
   (alcohol)

5. きせつ
   (season)

6. すそ
   (hemline)

Ⅲ Write the words below in *hiragana*.

1. *tasuke*
   (help)

2. *sasoi*
   (invitation)

3. *tsukue*
   (desk)

4. *osechi*
   (festive food)

5. *toshi*
   (age)

6. *aite*
   (partner)

第2課 2 Katakana (サ‐ト)
だいにか

(I) Practice writing the following ten *katakana* (サ through ト).

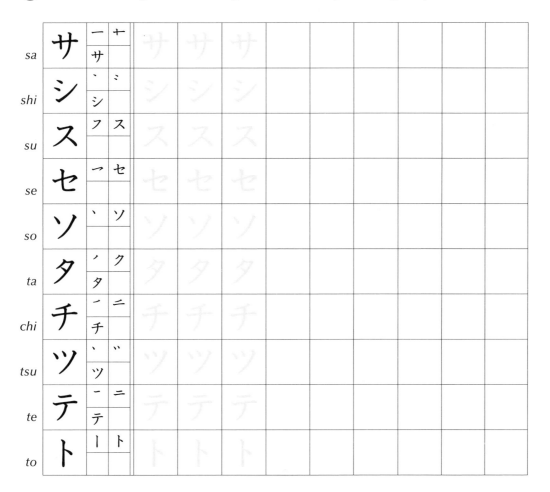

(II) Write the words below in *katakana.*

1. しーざー
   (Caesar)

2. すーつ
   (suit)

3. せっと
   (set)

4. そっくす
   (socks)

5. たこす
   (tacos)

6. ちーず
   (cheese)

7. たい
   (Thailand)

8. でっき
   (deck)

クラス _____ なまえ _____

第2課 3 Katakana (ナ‐ホ)
だい に か

Ⅰ Practice writing the following ten *katakana* (ナ through ホ).

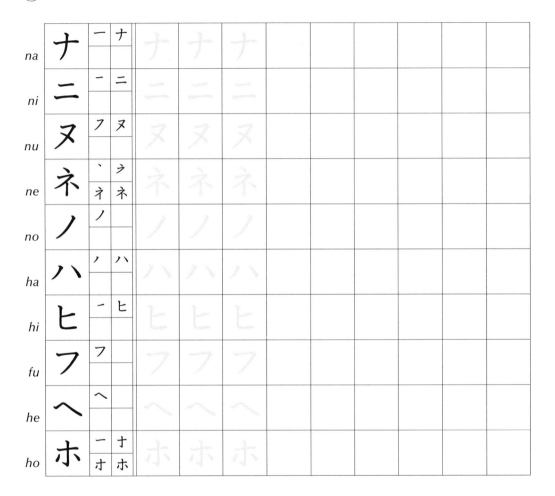

Ⅱ Write the words below in *katakana*.

1. ぼさのば
   (bossa nova)

2. かぬー
   (canoe)

3. はーぶ
   (herb)

4. びきに
   (bikinis)

5. なっつ
   (nuts)

6. ぺっと
   (pet)

7. こね
   (connection)

8. ひっぴー
   (hippie)

9. ねくたい
   (necktie)

第2課 だいにか 4 Katakana (マ - ヨ)

Ⅰ Practice writing the following eight *katakana* (マ through ヨ).

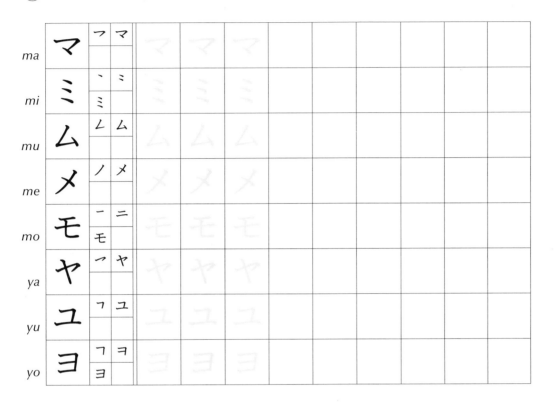

Ⅱ Write the words below in *katakana*.

1. めも
   (memo)

2. むーど
   (mood)

3. みに
   (mini)

4. まや
   (Maya)

5. よっと
   (yacht)

6. ゆーざー
   (user)

7. きゃっぷ
   (cap)

8. しちゅー
   (stew)

9. しょっく
   (shock)

クラス ＿＿＿＿＿＿＿＿ なまえ ＿＿＿＿＿＿＿＿＿＿＿＿＿

第2課 5 Katakana (ラ－ン)
だい に か

Ⅰ Practice writing the following eight *katakana* (ラ through ン).

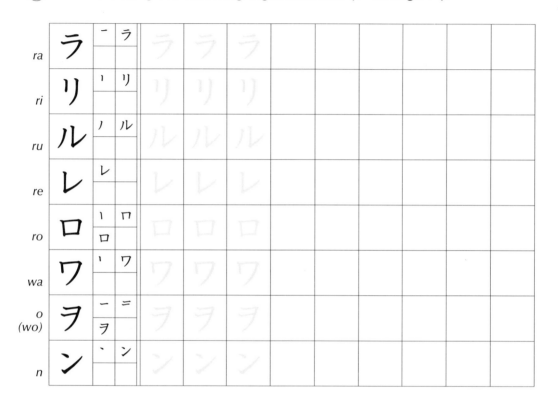

Ⅱ Write the words below in *katakana*.

The small *katakana* エ is used with シ and チ to transcribe the sounds "she" and "che": シェパード (shepherd), and チェンジ (change), for example.

1. よーろっぱ
(Europe)

2. わっくす
(wax)

3. るーれっと
(roulette)

4. あふりか
(Africa)

5. らーめん
(ramen noodle)

6. しぇーくすぴあ
(Shakespeare)

7. ちぇ・げばら
(Che Guevara)

クラス _____ なまえ _____

第**3**課 **1** Kanji Practice

001 一	一	一	一					
002 二	二	二	二					
003 三	三	三	三					
004 四	四	四	四					
005 五	五	五	五					
006 六	六	六	六					
007 七	七	七	七					
008 八	八	八	八					
009 九	九	九	九					
010 十	十	十	十					
011 百	百	百	百					
012 千	千	千	千					
013 万	万	万	万					
014 円	円	円	円					
015 時	時	時	時					

第3課 2 Using Kanji

(Ⅰ) Write the numbers in kanji.

1. 41

2. 300

3. 1,500

4. 2,890

5. 67,000

6. 128,000

7. 1,000,000

(Ⅱ) Write in kanji.

1. A：これはいくらですか。　　B：＿＿＿＿＿＿＿＿＿です。
　　　　　　　　　　　　　　　　　　 ろっぴゃくえん

2. A：いまなん＿＿＿ですか。　　B：＿＿＿＿＿＿＿＿です。
　　　　　　　　 じ　　　　　　　　　　　　 じゅうにじ

(Ⅲ) Using the kanji you have learned, translate the following sentences into Japanese.

1. This watch is 49,000 yen.

2. That bag is 5,300 yen.

3. Ms. Yamanaka gets up at six.

4. Ms. Kawaguchi goes to college at seven.

5. Mr. Suzuki usually goes to bed at about twelve.

6. I sometimes drink coffee at a cafe. The coffee is 180 yen.

クラス _____ なまえ _____

第4課 1 Kanji Practice

016	日	日	日	日					
017	本	本	本	本					
018	人	人	人	人					
019	月	月	月	月					
020	火	火	火	火					
021	水	水	水	水					
022	木	木	木	木					
023	金	金	金	金					
024	土	土	土	土					
025	曜	曜	曜	曜					
026	上	上	上	上					
027	下	下	下	下					
028	中	中	中	中					
029	半	半	半	半					

クラス _____   なまえ _____

第4課 2 Using Kanji

(I) Write in kanji.

1. Sunday   5. Thursday

2. Monday   6. Friday

3. Tuesday   7. Saturday

4. Wednesday

(II) Write in kanji.

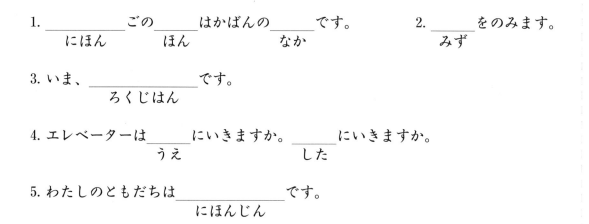

1. _____ごの_____はかばんの_____です。   2. _____をのみます。
    にほん   ほん   なか   みず

3. いま、_____です。
        ろくじはん

4. エレベーターは_____にいきますか。_____にいきますか。
            うえ   した

5. わたしのともだちは_____です。
            にほんじん

(III) Using the kanji you have learned, translate the following sentences into Japanese.

1. I went to a restaurant with a Japanese friend on Friday.

2. I got up at about ten thirty on Saturday.

3. I went to a temple alone on Monday.

4. The book is on the desk. The newspaper is under the book.

クラス _____　　なまえ _____

第5課 1 Kanji Practice

030	山	山	山	山					
031	川	川	川	川					
032	元	元	元	元					
033	気	気	気	気					
034	天	天	天	天					
035	私	私	私	私					
036	今	今	今	今					
037	田	田	田	田					
038	女	女	女	女					
039	男	男	男	男					
040	見	見	見	見					
041	行	行	行	行					
042	食	食	食	食					
043	飲	飲	飲	飲					

クラス _____   なまえ _____

第5課 2 Using Kanji

Ⅰ Write the appropriate mixes of kanji and *hiragana*.

1. _____ですか。
   げんき

2. _____はいい_____ですね。
   きょう   てんき

3. あの_____の_____は_____さんです。
   おとこ   ひと   やまかわ

4. あの_____の_____は_____さんです。
   おんな   ひと   やまだ

5. _____はきのうレストランに_____。
   わたし   いきました

6. ピザを_____。 コーヒーを_____。
        たべました   のみました

7. うちでテレビを_____。
              みました

Ⅱ Using the kanji you have learned, translate the following sentences into Japanese.

1. I am now in Japan.

2. Ms. Tanaka is fine. Mr. Yamakawa is not fine.

3. I went to the mountain with a Japanese man and woman.

4. I ate dinner with my friend on Tuesday.

5. On Wednesday, I drank a lot of alcohol. And then I saw a video.

クラス _____　なまえ _____

第6課 1 Kanji Practice

044	東	東	東	東						
045	西	西	西	西						
046	南	南	南	南						
047	北	北	北	北						
048	口	口	口	口						
049	出	出	出	出						
050	右	右	右	右						
051	左	左	左	左						
052	分	分	分	分						
053	先	先	先	先						
054	生	生	生	生						
055	大	大	大	大						
056	学	学	学	学						
057	外	外	外	外						
058	国	国	国	国						

クラス _____   *なまえ* _____

第6課 2 Using Kanji

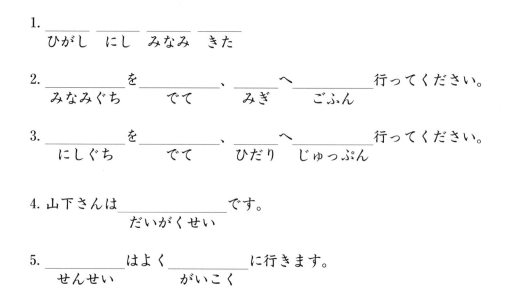

(I) Write the appropriate mixes of kanji and *hiragana*.

1. _____ _____ _____ _____
   ひがし   にし   みなみ   きた

2. _____を_____、_____へ_____行ってください。
   みなみぐち   でて   みぎ   ごふん

3. _____を_____、_____へ_____行ってください。
   にしぐち   でて   ひだり   じゅっぷん

4. 山下さんは_____です。
        だいがくせい

5. _____はよく_____に行きます。
   せんせい   がいこく

(II) Using the kanji you have learned, translate the following sentences into Japanese.

1. There are lots of foreign teachers in my college.

2. The college is to the left of a bank.

3. Go out the east exit and go to the right, please.

4. The restaurant is near the south exit.

5. I ate pizza and drank wine at the restaurant.

6. I waited for twenty minutes at the north exit.

クラス _____ なまえ _____

第7課 1 Kanji Practice

059	京	京	京	京						
060	子	子	子	子						
061	小	小	小	小						
062	会	会	会	会						
063	社	社	社	社						
064	父	父	父	父						
065	母	母	母	母						
066	高	高	高	高						
067	校	校	校	校						
068	毎	毎	毎	毎						
069	語	語	語	語						
070	文	文	文	文						
071	帰	帰	帰	帰						
072	入	入	入	入						

クラス _____　なまえ _____

第7課 2 Using Kanji

Ⓘ Write the appropriate mixes of kanji and *hiragana*.

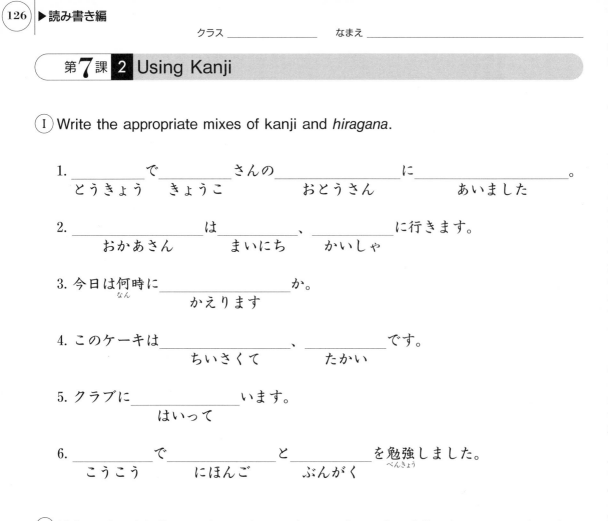

1. _____ で _____ さんの _____ に _____ 。
   とうきょう　　きょうこ　　　　　おとうさん　　　　　　あいました

2. _____ は _____ 、 _____ に行きます。
   おかあさん　　　　　まいにち　　　かいしゃ

3. 今日は何時に _____ か。
   　　　なん　　　　　かえります

4. このケーキは _____ 、 _____ です。
   　　　　　　　ちいさくて　　　　たかい

5. クラブに _____ います。
   　　　　はいって

6. _____ で _____ と _____ を勉強しました。
   こうこう　　　にほんご　　　　ぶんがく　　　　べんきょう

Ⓘ Using the kanji you have learned, translate the following sentences into Japanese.

1. Kyoko's younger sister is a high school student.

2. Kyoko's mother works for a small company.

3. Kyoko's father comes home late every day.

4. I am studying Japanese and literature.

5. Ms. Minami speaks English a little.

クラス _____ なまえ _____

第8課 1 Kanji Practice

073 員	員	員	員						
074 新	新	新	新						
075 聞	聞	聞	聞						
076 作	作	作	作						
077 仕	仕	仕	仕						
078 事	事	事	事						
079 電	電	電	電						
080 車	車	車	車						
081 休	休	休	休						
082 言	言	言	言						
083 読	読	読	読						
084 思	思	思	思						
085 次	次	次	次						
086 何	何	何	何						

クラス _____   なまえ _____

第8課 2 Using Kanji

Ⅰ Write the appropriate mixes of kanji and *hiragana*.

1. 川口さんは_____だと_____。
   かわぐち　　　　　かいしゃいん　　　　　　おもいます

2. 友だちは_____を_____と_____いました。
   とも　　　　　しごと　　　　やすむ　　　　いって

3. _____を_____。
   しんぶん　　　よみます

4. _____ _____を買いました。
   あたらしい　　　くるま　　か

5. _____の_____は_____ですか。
   つぎ　　　でんしゃ　　　　なんじ

6. _____の日にスパゲッティーを_____。
   やすみ　　　　　　　　　　　　　　つくりました

Ⅱ Translate the following sentences into Japanese.

1. I read the newspaper on a train.

2. I made a questionnaire.

3. I think company employees in Japan are busy.

4. What do you do on holidays?

5. Kyoko said that she went to Tokyo last week.

6. The next train comes at eleven o'clock.

クラス _____　　なまえ _____

第9課 1 Kanji Practice

087	午	午	午	午					
088	後	後	後	後					
089	前	前	前	前					
090	名	名	名	名					
091	白	白	白	白					
092	雨	雨	雨	雨					
093	書	書	書	書					
094	友	友	友	友					
095	間	間	間	間					
096	家	家	家	家					
097	話	話	話	話					
098	少	少	少	少					
099	古	古	古	古					
100	知	知	知	知					
101	来	来	来	来					

クラス _____   なまえ _____

第9課 2 Using Kanji

Ⅰ Write the appropriate mixes of kanji and *hiragana*.

1. _____ は _____ が降っていました。
　　　ごぜんちゅう　　　　あめ　　ふ

2. _____ は _____ の _____ に行って、_____。
　　　ごご　　　　　ともだち　　いえ　　　　　　　　　　はなしました

3. この _____ 着物は _____ _____ です。
　　　　しろい　きもの　　　　　すこし　　　　ふるい

4. あの人の _____ を _____ いますか。_____ ください。
　　　　　なまえ　　　　しって　　　　　　　　　かいて

5. _____ 待ちましたが、スーさんは _____。
　　　にじかん　　　　ま　　　　　　　　　　　　　　きませんでした

Ⅱ Translate the following sentences into Japanese.

1. I wrote a letter to my friend in the afternoon.

2. I read a book for one hour at home.

3. I had a talk with Ken's father. It was interesting.

4. The name of Mr. Yamashita's dog is Pochi.

5. My dictionary is a little old.

6. Please come to my house. Let's talk.

クラス _____ なまえ _____

第10課 1 Kanji Practice

102	住	住	住	住						
103	正	正	正	正						
104	年	年	年	年						
105	売	売	売	売						
106	買	買	買	買						
107	町	町	町	町						
108	長	長	長	長						
109	道	道	道	道						
110	雪	雪	雪	雪						
111	立	立	立	立						
112	自	自	自	自						
113	夜	夜	夜	夜						
114	朝	朝	朝	朝						
115	持	持	持	持						

クラス _____   なまえ _____

第10課 2 Using Kanji

Ⅰ Write the appropriate mixes of kanji and *hiragana*.

1. _____、この_____に_____つもりです。
   らいねん　　　　　　まち　　　　すむ

2. _____の_____に_____が降りました。
   ことし　　　　おしょうがつ　　　ゆき　　　ふ

3. _____の時計を_____、友だちのプレゼントを_____。
   じぶん　　とけい　　　　うって　　　　　　　　　　　　　　　かいました

4. _____におじぞうさんが_____います。
   みち　　　　　　　　　たって

5. あしたの_____、かさを_____きてください。
   あさ　　　　　　　もって

6. _____が_____なりました。
   よる　　　ながく

Ⅱ Translate the following sentences into Japanese.

1. I live in a small town.

2. It snowed yesterday morning.

3. I sold my old car and bought a new one.

4. Ms. Yamada is tall and has long hair.

5. Do you have an umbrella?

6. This road becomes quiet at night.

クラス _____ なまえ _____

第11課 1 Kanji Practice

手	手	手	手						
紙	紙	紙	紙						
好	好	好	好						
近	近	近	近						
明	明	明	明						
病	病	病	病						
院	院	院	院						
映	映	映	映						
画	画	画	画						
歌	歌	歌	歌						
市	市	市	市						
所	所	所	所						
勉	勉	勉	勉						
強	強	強	強						
有	有	有	有						
旅	旅	旅	旅						

クラス _____   なまえ _____

第11課 2 Using Kanji

Ⅰ Write the appropriate mixes of kanji and *hiragana*.

1. 友だちから_____をもらいました。とても_____人です。
　　　　　　てがみ　　　　　　　　　　　　　あかるい

2. _____を見たり、_____して、日本語を_____します。
　　えいが　　　　　　　うたったり　　　　　　　　べんきょう

3. 家の_____に_____があります。
　　　ちかく　　びょういん

4. 父は_____が_____です。
　　　りょこう　　すき

5. 鎌倉_____に住んでいます。とても_____な_____です。
　かまくら　し　　　　　　　　　　ゆうめい　　ところ

Ⅱ Translate the following sentences into Japanese.

1. On my days off I watch movies and sing songs and so on.

2. My friend lives in my neighborhood.

3. I traveled to various places.

4. I don't want to go to a hospital tomorrow.

5. I want to become famous in the future.

6. Please write a letter to me.

7. I have never studied foreign languages.

クラス _____ なまえ _____

第12課 1 Kanji Practice

132 昔	昔	昔	昔					
133 々	々	々	々					
134 神	神	神	神					
135 早	早	早	早					
136 起	起	起	起					
137 牛	牛	牛	牛					
138 使	使	使	使					
139 働	働	働	働					
140 連	連	連	連					
141 別	別	別	別					
142 度	度	度	度					
143 赤	赤	赤	赤					
144 青	青	青	青					
145 色	色	色	色					

クラス _____　なまえ _____

第12課 2 Using Kanji

Ⅰ Write the appropriate mixes of kanji and *hiragana*.

1. _____、ある所に_____がいました。
　　むかしむかし　　　　　　　　かみさま

2. _____を_____、_____います。
　　うし　　　　つかって　　　　はたらいて

3. 毎日、朝_____、_____。
　　　　　　はやく　　　　おきます

4. 大人は_____ ____、子どもは_____ ____のＴシャツを着ています。
　　おとな　あかい　　いろ　　　　　　　あおい　　いろ　　ティー　　　　き

5. _____の休みに、友だちを_____ _____。
　　こんど　　　　　　　　　　　つれて　　　　かえります

6. そこで、友だちと_____。
　　　　　　　　　わかれました

Ⅱ Translate the following sentences into Japanese.

1. I like red color and blue color.

2. Let's go to a movie in the near future.

3. I don't like getting up early in the morning.

4. I don't want to separate from you.

5. May I use a telephone?

6. I have to work this weekend.